LIFE SPAN
A Collection of Poetry

By Deanna Repose Oaks

TABLE OF CONTENTS

FORWARD

This journey you are about to embark on will reveal feelings of new love, old love, and the emotional wreckage that comes as a result. Explorations of family life and friendships will be had, without the rose-colored glasses. Cultural observations are followed by nature poems – because you can't just look at one side of the coin.

A book of poems, once assembled, does not seem like a big deal to read because there are less pages (and words) than a novel. But, when you consider how many stories are told in just under 12,000 words, well, it is overwhelming. Prepare yourself accordingly.

One last note before I let you read to your hearts content – I don't use a lot of punctuation in my poems. I let the rhythm of the spoken words and the breaks in the lines punctuate for me. When you read, read aloud, these are best when voiced!

DEDICATION

This book is dedicated to Trayce, Vicki, and Sharon – for your unrelenting belief in me. To my husband for supporting me. To Bill, Bryan, Alex, Barbara and Dana, as well as all the new members of PCWG of Georgia for making me the poet I am today.

LIFE SPAN

A life-span of a car is longer than its first broken
    part
Just as a life-span of a person is longer than its
    first broken heart

What I have learned within mine
Maybe could
Be applied to yours

Just feel these words
In the order they appeal
Rather than in their pours

You might find something I didn't
Amongst the pain
And the reflections

Superseding any of my silly thoughts
Of how you should see it
With my inflections

Because living within mine can never be yours
But seeing mine may help you live through
    yours

NEW LOVE

WE'RE NOT IN KANSAS ANYMORE

I feel like Dorothy
Between Kansas and Oz
Stuck in a tornado
Whirling without pause
I feel safe here
Within the wind
Knowing my adventure
Is about to begin
I am not holding back
But reaching for the sky
Grabbing for the rainbow
Aiming really high
I know Oz is out there
I read so in books
I just want to see so
And have one look
When this wind came along
I jumped in
Hoping it would take me
Along within
Now I am floating
Through the sky
Floating toward Oz
Way up so high
I want to ensure
This isn't a dream
And I won't wake up
Where everything will seem
So bland and empty
Hollow and bare
Like the Kansas I left
Before I cared

MELTING HEARTS

Defenses once put in place
Failed to work that night
I want to question why
Yet this just feels too right
I forget to ask
Then sit and bask
In an intimacy greater than I've ever felt

Words cannot express how I feel
Because it's strong but yet unreal
As we talk and share our thoughts
We grow closer, I am caught
Soon, I know, my heart will melt

AT LAST

Hearing you say you missed me, like I missed
    you
Hurt somehow
I feel it could have been avoided, if I'd just told
    you...
It's passed now
I felt so much when we were one
I didn't dare say
I felt you would pass me by
Walk away
I know you didn't leave me
When we parted ways
We both changed our lives
I didn't ask you to stay
I couldn't ask if you wanted me
As much as I wanted you
I couldn't ask "what if...."
Because I thought you knew
When you left, I thought for good
I ached for you to return
Now in my life again
I'm afraid of the burn
I'm lost in emotions
Almost about to cry
I know I can't go back
Even though I want to try
Afraid to share the feelings I feel
Since the time that's passed
Now that you are here again
I feel better at last....

MY WORRY

The wind whips my hair across my face;
His cologne mingles with my perfume there.
Memories of what we've done -
Dreams of what's to come -
Dance through my thoughts
While a smile plays on my lips.
There is so much still unknown,
Even with the certainty I feel,
To define what all this means.
My smile broadens with a single thought:
My worry is gone.

The Perfect Woman

The perfect woman at your side
Has some flaws that she'll hide
It isn't that she's not right
It's just her secret is out of sight
Her mirror is warped enough to mask
All the questions you'll never ask
What lies beneath the "perfect" shell
Is a tangled, tormented web of hell
Whose fury has yet to be unleashed
Or whose darkest secrets are yet released
There are times she wants the dam to break
But knows too well of that mistake
So she keeps her flaws locked away
Hiding from the light of day
Because there are things you shouldn't see
 All of her, or all of me.

Under Perfect Light

He gazed upon me in perfect light
Amazed and enthralled by the sight
But could he see into the depths
Where my tortured soul is kept?
The depths are deep, but the path is clear
As the path is paved with fear
Alluding to what does scare
While speaking of the things I care
Was all I did that faithful night
While I stood under perfect light

On a Perfect Night

We met for dinner on a perfect night
One that started things off right
Our food was filling and hit the spot
While we spoke of things naught
The walk we then took through town
Had both its ups and its downs
The dark sky sparkled with stars
And hid all my hideous scars
But at the end of the perfect night
Dawned a new day with morning light
Revealing the perfect woman under perfect light on perfect night
Wasn't so perfect after all.

OPEN INVITATION

The bedroom door once locked
Is now open wide
I stand on the threshold
Hesitant to go inside

As memories of his touch
Skate across my skin
I allow myself
To think thoughts full of sin
While I stand in the doorway
With my body on fire
I reign myself back
Hold onto my desire
My emotions run deep
Below all the lust
I want to forsake them
But I'm afraid to trust
That I can walk out
After I've gone in
Because I know his true love
I can't win.

WHAT I'M THINKING

He wants to know:
Thoughts in my head.
Those twisted things
So filled with dread.
Do I share every one,
Let him see the fear?
Do I tell him everything,
Even things I hold dear?
My first thought is "yes"
Even though it should be "no"
For telling him everything,
Giving him too much to know
May give him too much to throw
Back at me.

IT HAPPENED @ CAMBRIA PINES LODGE
(Around 1:30 PM on April 24, 2004)

I try to relate to your world
But I don't know where I stand
I'm trying to define my world
While holding onto your hand
Since your doubts became known
I have felt fear
I don't know where this will end
Or where to go from here
I try to ease my mind
But I can't seem to ask
Will the world change too soon
Or will it want to last?
I think you felt too much
And pulled yourself back
Or is there some other knowledge
That I seem to lack?

DINNER TONIGHT?

The resolve in your voice
When you say no
Cuts like a knife
Even though
Your heart hurts as much as mine
By the absence we share

The hurt in my heart
When I hear no
Won't go away
Even though
My head tells my heart the truth
"You would never dare"

Hurt me in the way you did
By using the words that bit
They were just the words you said
To express conflict
Schedules, distance, a complete lack of time
Not your fault
Not mine

I have to remember I'm a little ahead
We don't yet stand side by side
There are things I feel, thoughts I have
That I still have to hide
I have to remember to wait a while
Until we stand side by side
You aren't going anywhere I'm not
But neither am I

FLIRTING

Does he flirt, or is it me?
Does he flirt because of me?
How's a girl supposed to know,
When the guy doesn't show?

She's got questions (confusion and doubts
     abound)
She wants to ask, but he's not around.
He's got a life that she can't see –
All he is is a mystery.

She feels he started this little dance,
That's why she decided to take the chance.
Now that he didn't show
She feels she'll never know:

Was he flirting or was it a game?
Is she the one who is lame?
Did she read him wrong, or was she right
About the way it went that night?

HOPING

I'm starting over again, soon
Hoping the next one won't swoon
Or think I'm perfect (I'm not)
Or diss me once I'm caught
I expect these things from past
All the ones that didn't last
This time I'm playing a different game
Hoping the next one isn't lame
Watching them and all their tricks
Using them and their pricks
If they don't play it right
Count them out; take flight
No use in getting myself in
Hoping the next one will win:
       My heart (that breaks too easily)
       My mind (that always knows)
       My soul (that bruises easy)
       My love (that always grows)

FATAL KISS

Falling in love, don't know what to say,
I'm falling faster every single day.
The more of him that he shows,
The more my love for him grows.
His kindness, understanding and daring
Underneath it all the undying caring,
Does he love me, or does he not?

Now I know I'm caught.
I'm so stuck and can't get out.
The words I say I'll always doubt.
I know there's no use to hide,
Yet I lock my feelings inside.
So no one can see them, no one can say,
That I'm out just to get my way.
When I looked into his eyes-
All the pretending became such lies,

Now, all that's left is a fatal kiss
And to get it is my last wish.

WORDS YOU SAY

When you speak to me
The world falls away
I don't remember anything
But the words you say
I look around, the world is gone
There is only you talking to me

The words you spoke to me
Made the world fall dead
Now I can't remember
The words you said
I look around, there is nothing to see
You are gone, nowhere near me
It seems they were just words you said
To get into my heart; into my bed.

FAMILY LIFE

TOBACCO SMOKE

I could almost see the wisp
Curling around his bald head
Leather chair, soft, smooth, worn
The small table, at arm's length
The tray filled with ash
Pipe in his mouth
Glasses on the bridge of his nose
Book in his hand
Almost, not quite
On my tongue the question
Almost asked
A knowing smile crosses my face
"Excuse me"
And just as fast, it's gone
      "Sorry, I thought I smelt something
      burning."

READING WILLS

The cash rolls in
"For you, you and you
But not you"
The lawyer says
"These people belong here
You don't"
I am not fooled by the smile he shows
Because behind his back is a knife he stows
Soon it will be buried deep
So deep I should not feel
Paralyzed by the blade
Conquered by its steel
Per the instructions

He smiles because he doesn't know me
Or the people I choose to love
I never cared for this cash
These inflictions cannot hurt me
I love only the good I choose to see
Even with a blade in my back
For I know that beneath it all
It is love the both they lacked
So let the cash roll in for them, them, and them
Not me
I don't need it you see
For all I ever cared about is
The love I give; always free

LIFE TO LEAD

I have no faith in what I do
Those who believe are so few
My parents disregard all I say
"Make your dreams another day"
They tied me down in iron chains
And during my parade they reign
I try to get out of this mess
But am surrounded by loneliness
What can I do? – forget it
This way I'll never regret it
But I have my life to live
And to myself I will give
A chance to fulfill my dreams
Living a life to total extremes.

MISCARRIAGE

Cramps bring pain to a child mother
Alone in a hospital room
Drugs given to no avail
The baby met a dreadful doom
An unplanned error
The child survived the pain
The remedy is not so well
Her heart, now stained
She couldn't tell if she was loved
The dad of the baby was there
Parents, unseen by the child
The baby seemed so unfair
This ordeal was a tragedy
Wanted to take her last breath
There are no apron strings to clutch at
No block to be a chip off of
There is no way of ever knowing
If there was any love
Blood is bled, and tears are cried
Everything except for life to the baby that died
She can't forget the instinct
To keep her baby from being extinct.

WEIGHT IN GOLD

Locked inside their house as lonely as can be
Looking out a window through a reflection of me
Silent, empty streets with the skies so gray
Seems no one is happy enough on this day
Silent tears start falling from my eyes
From far away I hear painful cries
Later that night I hear a sob, a scream
Realizing it's me, awaking from a dream
Then I cry, then I sleep
And know, then, why I weep
Every dream is such a bitter pill
Every morning awaking only to feel
Scared, angry and even sad
Stay here any longer, I'll go mad
I see a mirror as I leave
Catch a reflection that makes me heave
Loneliness captured and held me prisoner
Fear of the unknown can no longer hinder
My escape from a box like a mime
I kept silent, was patient with time
Becoming elated as I walk the street
Knowing with enthusiasm I can greet
Every day with something new
Freedom found beyond their purview
Realizing that I now can hold
Happiness worth its weight in gold.

DAD

As I drive through the streets,
I am reminded of you.
You taught me how to read maps
To get me where I need to go.

As I receive change after spending money,
I am reminded of you.
You taught me how to earn money
Then save my nickels and dimes.

As I turn my lights off,
I am reminded of you.
You taught me how to fix light fixtures
So that I would never be in the dark.

As I get my oil changed,
I am reminded of you.
You taught me how to care for my car
And keep mechanics from ripping me off.

As I rinse vegetables,
I am reminded of you.
You taught me how to pull weeds
To keep the flowers and veggies healthy.

As I cook dinner,
I am reminded of you.
You taught me cook with an iron skillet
Over a fire and on the stove.

As I go about my day, every day,
I am reminded of you.
You taught me how to live in the world,

How to care for others
How to care for myself
How to be.

OLD LOVE

MOVING DAY

I am haunting my past
Before it haunts me
Checking for ghosts
Quite stealthily
Making sure I don't leave behind
Something I forgot
Before I move to something great
And leave behind the lot
But every time I look back
My sadness grows
Because I want to leave it all
It's so full of woes
The little bits I want to take
Lose meaning every day
And every time I redefine
I lose what could make me stay.

SCREWED (AND LIKING IT)

The last guy I screwed loved me
The last guy I loved screwed me

I can't win.

OUR NIGHT

You'd think I'd be happy because
You remembered our night
And I was fine, I really was
Until my thoughts took flight

I used to think I was the only one
That remembered that night so well
Now I see the other side, I'm stunned
And my life has gone to hell.

Every touch, every move
Makes me ache for something more
Holds something I can't approve
Reminds me of what I felt before

The nights we spoke on the phone
Conversations through the night
Intimacy I thought I felt alone
Moments that disappeared, gone

To speak of this to you I cannot
It would hurt me more today
Yet I must reveal this before I am caught
And never speak of it after this day.

FORGIVE ME, PLEASE

Forgive me please
For not letting you talk
Forgive me please
For not picking up the phone
Forgive me please
For not wanting to push
Forgive me PLEASE
For being an emotional wreck

My urge was to just show up
Without your permission
I didn't want to just push myself on you
To have you dismiss me
So, I asked, waited for an answer
Didn't get one
Asked again, "I don't know. I just don't know."
Didn't ask again

I just did what I always do
Became strong
Overcame my feelings of rejection
You didn't know something was wrong
ON PURPOSE
My fault, I know
Not communicating right
Not knowing how
Not wanting to be vulnerable, unable, weepy
Not able to ask again, differently
Forgive me?

PEP TALK FROM HELL

Here I am at the bottom of my abyss
Looking up for the light
There you are on the precipice
Thinking what you did was right
Shine your light down towards me
So I can get myself out
I don't want you to climb down
If you do, we will bout
I'm a big girl, the climb won't be hard
It's just so dark, and it looks so far
I hear you say the light's on it's way
But it has yet to come
I need your actions without delay
Or I will fall and succumb
To the numb blackness surrounding
The steady emptiness compounding
The solace I found because of you.

HAVING SAID NOTHING

It is called the silent treatment
When nothing is said
But it is clearly known
That anger is being fed
Anger that walked in the door
Unexplained, exploded
No reason why
The world imploded
There is nothing to say
So silence prevails
Until the storm ends
And the ship sails
Yet the storm rages on
Within the silent mess
Because of the silence
So much added stress
Slamming doors
Thrown things
Childish anger
Silence brings

RED TRUCK

The red truck crashed through my dreams
    (again)
Haunting me still
It isn't what it seems
I hate how I feel
In my dreams the crash
Is full of death and rot
My life has since changed
My view has not
I was left in the dust
And debris of what was
Reminders of it hurts
Mainly because
Breaking glass and exploding bags
Can't be repaired
Though in my dreams
They have been dared
Crashing through my life
Again and again over time
I want it to go away
I want it here, I'm....
The red truck changed my life
Against my will
Every once in a while it haunts my dreams
Still

CHEMISTRY CLASS

I sat at the table
Trying to find
A definition of what I want
In your kind
I guess it all boils down
To the chemistry
That's supposed to happen
Between you and me
Somehow though it isn't there
The math isn't right
I tried to force it
But I don't want to fight
I want it to be there
Without the work
For both of us equally
Without a berth
I'll take the A Bomb
Even with the decay
Because I want it
To blow me away
I want someone with a spark
That catches fire
Someone who won't burn
But'll fan the flames higher
As I tried to define
This little spark
I realized it has to be
Something in the heart
Of the person across from me
When I looked again
It still wasn't there
But how do I tell you
And still be fair?

MIND MADE UP

You complain to me of being alone
After you violently shoved me away
You sit there wanting me back
After throwing me out that day
I wonder what changed you
From being alone
To lonely
And what will happen to me
When you figure out
That what you want isn't me
Again
I can't face that truth today
Not after what I've been through
So I need to leave you alone
Thinking "What have I done?"

I still see the white walls painted red
In the house that should have been mine
And I wonder what it would be like
If you hadn't changed your mind
But what is past has passed
And there is no going back
To find the treasures we left behind
Or the relationship that we now lack

WHEN I SEE YOU AGAIN

Echoes of what you didn't say
Ring through my ears
I can't seem to shake them
Even as night draws near
Memories of how you felt
Flow over my skin
I can't seem to shake them
But I don't want to win
I want to hear what you didn't say
And feel your touch anew
Please don't worry how I'll be
Or what I may say or do
I feel you cannot scare me
Even if you try

Echoes of what you did say
Ring through my ears
I can't seem to shake them
Even as the end draws near
Memories of how it felt
Pierce through my skin
I can't seem to stop them
But there is no way to win
I didn't want to hear what you said
Or have my heart split in two
Please don't worry how it'll be
Now that it's said and done
I feel you cannot scare me
Even if you try

It ended so quickly
It didn't even begin
But I felt it all

Because I fell all the way in
How will it be when I see you again?

THIS BOY I KNEW

Once upon a time I knew
This boy who loved me through & through
    But that was just a lie

And every time I think of him
All I want is to be with him
    But that leads to good-bye

So I sit and ponder many things
And hope and hope the phone rings
    But that boy won't say hi

It seems his love for me was never there
And it was a fake love affair
    But that won't help my love die.

SEXUAL DRIVE

Learning to drive a stick shift
Knowing when to engage the clutch
Putting the car in gear
Getting the car from first to second
Second to third
Third to fourth
Fourth into fifth
Then reverse, the most important but least used
Learning to avoid stalling out
When stopping and starting
Or turning around, infrequently
Starting on neighborhood streets
Gaining confidence, learning the city
Moving onto the interstate
Cruising through the country
Seeing the sights
      Peaks and valleys
      Deserts and lakes
Always moving, ahead
Second nature, but exciting still
Each time the key is turned.

BUILDING A FUTURE

It began the moment our eyes first met
That very first night
I became yours; you became mine
Seamlessly; without fright
With every moment of every day
Comes with it a greater appreciation
For what you have done for me
Without all the complication
I sit and revel in all I know
About you and your past
And the one thing that I can't help think
Is this is my "At Last"
I am relieved I know you
And all your pain
Because I know there is so much
The two of us can gain
And every moment from that moment on
The foundation gets stronger still
Soon we can build our future
Together, always, we will

EMOTIONAL

WRECKAGE

FEELING DOWN

Just as you are feeling at your worst
Someone may make your day
It may come at a time you won't like
But give it a chance, hear what they say
For the message may hold power
Beyond your belief
So a "horrible inconvenience"
Could be quite the relief
Let your fences fall
From the stresses of life
Enjoy those around you
It will help you through strife
Hear the love behind the anger
And laughter beyond tears
Give as much as you take
Float through your years

VERTIGO

The world is spinning out of control
I want it to stop, or at least to slow
Can't focus on what's in front of me
The spin is too fast for me to see
Anxiety grows, fear fast on its heels
Room spinning faster, as if on wheels
The floor falls out from beneath my feet
Soon, gravity and I are destined to meet
Until then, I spin, trying to hold on
To something real, but it is beyond
Beyond anything within my reach
Oh please stop spinning, to the world I beseech!

CONCRETE

Anger has built inside of you,
Because of what isn't through.
A lunacy erodes your thoughts;
By and by your dead dream rots.
To survive, you split in two,
Wanting to escape, no knowing to.
An argument is inside of thee,
To satisfy it, you try to flee.
A bridge over water is then found.
You jump and land underground.
The escape desired is now complete –
Your name is engraved in concrete.

FAILING MISERABLY

Can't sleep for all the stress
Looking around, everything a mess
Undone things left here and there
Uncalled friends, all too aware
Of how I am and all I do
My intentions, non-actions, follow through
Can't help where I am or how I got
This situation, all I've caught
Now I see and I can't fix
The mess I am now amidst
So the deeper in I go
To try to reap what I sow
Keeping in mind, that should I fail
At least I tried before the hammer hit the nail

ROAD BLOCKS

Sometimes you just need a roadblock
To keep you from doing
That really stupid something,
The one that will be screwing
You for the rest of your life
The roadblock blocks your path
And keeps you in the clear
It holds back the wrath
Of the evil thing you could do
Or the stupid thought
It keeps you out of harms way
And from being caught
So why be angry
For something in the way
It could just be the one thing
That just saved the day

OUTSIDE CHAIR

Bright orange chair
In front of a deep black door
Sitting alone atop a staircase
Waiting for someone
Something
Anything at all
A strong wind
A tired dancer
A few flurries of snow
Maybe even some activity below
Keeping a vigil
Without patience
Just consequence
Rust

VERY, VERY BAD THING

Shut it down
Shut it out
I can't take it
Without a doubt
There is such a thing
As too much feeling
I feel it now
I hate it
Shut it out
I can't take it
There is more
I just know
But I can't see
Need to let go
But I can't
Shut it down
Shut it out
It is everywhere
It is everything
That is wrong
With this world
Rolled up in one
Very, Very bad thing.

BOUQUET OF ROSES

Laying by the roadside
Amidst shards of glass
Was a bouquet of roses
White, beautiful, and still fresh
Seeming like a bride's bouquet
Discarded on an exit ramp
They looked out of place there
As if stripped from their owner
Rather than left as a gift
For someone else to find
Taken by tragedy,
Left by consequence,
Observed by chance?
As I drove past them
I gave pause
What if those were mine?

NEW DAY

I arrive alone
Leave the same way
Hoping all the while
For a new day
One that will bring change
Discouraged, sure, but not giving in
I'm not letting this life win
All I want is for a new one to begin
Desire prevails and drives me on
Seeing how others have won
Watching as they all have fun
Knowing it could all be mine
A new life, one that fits fine
Even if it's hard to find

ACQUAINTENANCES

Transparent
Transient
The wanderers through our lives
Never stay for long
They change you in ways never expected
They hurt you in ways unavoidable
They strengthen you in ways unimaginable
Moments as ships passing at sea
Memories like ice cream in summer
Melting with time
Dripping, staining, yet no longer edible
Your reflection changed forever by their mirror
You know they were there
With what little proof you have
You try to hold on
The idea of who you once were – faded
Replaced by who you now are
Because the wanderers have been there
Transparent
Transient

BAD MOOD

Demanding, bitchy and otherwise mad
Wishing, hoping for things not so bad
Hurting, hungry, needing something more
Flirting, smiling, trying like before
Pushing people beyond being kind
Needing answers before their time
Stop this please, before this ends
On its own, it won't mend

NOT LETTING GO

I'm not who I want to be
But not for lack of trying
I finally figured out
Why I feel I'm lying
Back then things were a dream
It was all unreal
I let it all out
I allowed myself to feel
When life turned ugly
And love became untrue
I locked myself inside
So the hurt wouldn't undo
All the dreams I dreamt
Or all the things I felt
I held on tight, kept it close
Hoping the memories wouldn't melt
Holding on is now hurting more
Than if I could let go
So now I'm doing that
Moving on, past what I know

SAD POTATO

Who knew I would be denied the fries
And the chips
No hash browns for me
Mashed taken away without my say
Nothing out of the oven covered in cheese
Never twice baked
Or scalloped so very cute
I am just a plain potato
So sad in my skin
I just want to be cut open and flayed
Into something beautiful, desired
Something worthy of magazine covers
Celebrity chefs
Anything but this big brown sack

A MOMENT

Can change your life
If you let it
Can change your heart
If you feel it
Can change your mind
If you think about it
> Passion is living in the moment
> That changes you
> Hopeless in my passion
> The moments compounding, shoving me around
> Changing me without control
Most people don't understand
There is too much change
Too much unknown
> To give in – too much
Wanting someone out there
That changes as I do – please give me hope
For so long, searching to no avail
Salvation so far away
> Give me a moment
> I will change your heart
> Give me a moment
> I will show you my world
> Give me a moment
> I will give it back to you.

CROSSING THE LINE

Two white crosses
Embedded in the greenest grasses
Between the blacktop lanes
Just beyond the yellow lines
Crossed
Warnings from the white gauges
And the red reflectors
Just before the blue lights pulsate
Two white crosses
Embedded

CURRENTLY WORKING

Sitting at my desk
Watching the hours tick by
So far from home
Time doesn't fly
Wanting to earn cash
So I keep this job sustained
Just not enough tasks
To keep me entertained
I know I should be grateful
For every check that I earn
But this boredom may overtake me
Enough that bridges will soon burn
I instead focus on my goals
Working for the man
To keep the roof over my head
And the gun out of my hand

BRIGHT SIDE

It is broken
Bent
Burned
But it wasn't alive
(bright side)
It was lost
Beaten
Shunned
But it wasn't dead
(bright side)
There is always
(bright side)
Even if you can't see it
(dark side)
Have faith it is there
(bright side)
Before you give in or up
(dark side)
It is easier to wallow
(dark side)
Brightness can be overwhelming
(dark side)
But even in the dark, there is light
(bright side)
As long as you bring it with you

LOVE & COFFEE STAINS

The pages turn as the wind sweeps over
I stand quickly
Not wanting to lose my place
Too quickly
The table wobbles
The coffee spills
I weep as I wipe
Blindly plopping towels
On spots
Puddles
Through the tears
Wishing I could take it back
Make it whole again
As it dries
Warped
Emotion held captive
I cry again
Reminded of the wind
Sweeping the pages
Forever marking my place
My presence staining
The truest of loves

FRIENDSHIP

CRACKED

A building standing empty along the lot.
Friends speaking of honesty within the thought
A crack was noticed in the building facade,
A coincidence, rather odd.
Reminiscing of a life a bit cracked,
As was the discussion of the past.
The building is still standing along the lot,
Empty, broken, and for now forgot.
Yet there will be a day when it is seen
And someone will fix it, make it clean.

THE PATH AND NOTHING MORE

The surface tension of sexual desire has never
    been broken,
Even though it has been tested every time I
    speak your name, hear your voice, or see
    your face.
The tension, interlaced with an indescribable
    connection, has formed into a bond,
A bond wrapped with friendship and a strong
    desire to see you healthy, happy, and
    whole,
All coiled together tightly with sexual tension
    that has never been broken.
As intense as it sounds, there is a level of
    comfort and trust there,
A level so high, silence, stillness, and distance
    do not distort it.
I wonder constantly why we aren't more than we
    are today:
Which words I could have used to express it,
Which actions I could have taken to show it,
What match I could have lit to spark it.
Every time I wonder, a time comes when I must
    step into my reality,
A reality that tells me I am ridiculous to think
    this way, of a man I barely know,
A man I see on a path of self-destruction.
Then I realize I can't follow that path, without
    hurting,
And there I find the reason the words aren't
    there, the actions held back, the match
    unused.
It is the path and nothing more.

My own path is laid in stone, purposefully,
      unyielding in direction at times.
There seems to be a pattern between my path
      and yours: they frequently meet at
      crossroads.
Each time I approach you at a crossroad, I again
      realize I can't follow without hurting.
Your path is rough, rocky, and sometimes
      impassible.
I have been on that path with others, almost lost
      my life there once.
I can't go that way again, no matter how strong
      the desire.
As I watch you walk your path without me, I
      realize I can love you:
It is the path and nothing more.

While I cannot follow you on your path, or force
      you to switch paths, or beg you to take
      mine,
Our bond transcends our divergent paths,
It will bring us together in any time of need,
No matter how far apart our paths are, or the
      dangers the bond must overcome.
I will be there to rescue you from the
      destruction, should you need me.
After all, it is a path and nothing more.

FRIENDSHIP REKINDLED

Fear of the anger that was once bestowed
Became an electric fence
Where a zillion amps flowed
The fence now gone, destroyed
As if never there
Making us question why we avoid
Our friendship once so strong
Can be that way again
It won't even take that long

Once we decided, it was if no time had passed
Our friendship just as it was
When we saw each other last

MENDING FENCES

The fence once put in place
Is falling into disrepair
Left to ponder if it should be fixed
Or if it should be moved somewhere
Far removed from you
In order to rekindle friendship
Our lives have changed so much
There is no longer the hardship
That our friendship couldn't endure
In it's place this sadness
Loss of friendship so pure
Wanting to move the fence
Is first step towards more
Are you be willing to help me
Or do you still abhor
The honesty I gave to you
Which you asked of me that day
Asking if you wanted truth
Or wanted me to say
What you wanted to hear
Then there is the fence
I built to keep you out
It was my best defense
Against the pain I couldn't fix
The pain you were living
I couldn't help, couldn't face
Couldn't be that forgiving
All I wanted was more for you
Than the ache you embrace
You did what you needed to do
I did the same
Wondering now, as I attempt to mend this fence
Do you still hold me to blame?

SEA OF PINK

On Thursday night I waded into a sea of pink
Not caring what anyone else would think
Knowing that people in the drink
Do more than wear the color pink
They swim upstream even as all seems lost,
As hopes and dreams are dashed and tossed.
They fight this fight, and will until it is won.
They swim and swim until it is swum.
As friends, family and strangers falter, flail and
        sometimes drown
The pink tides raise them higher, floating over
        rocky ground.
As Friday morning came around,
This sea of pink was more profound,
Winding its way from solid stone,
20 long miles until it hits home.
The sea of pink surges with a tide,
Held within every pink shade, in every pink
        stride.
Saturday morning dawned anew.
This sea of pink took on a deeper hue,
Crashing waves 20 miles further upon the
        beach.
By nightfall children play within its reach.
The sea of pink closed this night,
Dancing its dance under pale pink light.
Sunday begins as tent city goes down.
The sea of pink starts moving the crowd.
Tales are regaled of what we have done:
20 more miles, the pain, the trouble and fun,
Of the fight we just fought and all it will do,
The sea of pink describes its every hue.
Wading in swimming along with the crowd,

Walking 60 miles over unsure ground,
I feel what I have done; I am so proud.

BROKEN FAUCET

Screaming, yelling, fighting mad
At the faucet broken bad
Spending money for the fix
Expenses not in the mix
Hiding cleansers from baby's hands
Ignoring swearing, following demands
(*!@$*!*** water everwhere, get the mop
Wait $*@$ no make the water stop!!!)
It is just a broken faucet after all
Just some plumbing taken a fall
Water floating under the bridge
(Well, actually across the floor, then under the
        fridge)
It is all good now, fixed up nice
Not bad for a night's work, twice!

BIRTHDAY SURPRISE

Having lunch with a dear friend
The kind of lunch that doesn't want to end
When in walks a group of cackly ladies
Loud, happy, little older than babies
These ladies were bubbly about the day
A surprise, a celebration, a little par-tay!
Their cackle took over, but pleasantly so
Because the birthday girl had such a radiant
    glow
As we ate we couldn't help but awe
At the gathering, a great hurrah
Both looking on, just hoping we could be
Just like these ladies at the age they be

FROM HERE

My heart has been here since the beginning
You've just arrived today
I've waited long, but I didn't forget you
I just don't remember where I was going
A new direction is needed

I ask you because you are here
Not because your answer will change
What I've already decided
But you might have a better idea
Than anything I can dream

Your opinion will not change me
Although it may change my path
But only if I want it to, not because of you

I hope you hear what I am saying
As well as understand what I am feeling
Because it means more to me
Than where I am going

AMIDST YOUR LIFE & FRIENDS

By telling me to ignore
Or that it didn't mean a thing
Can't diminish what I gained
Or come close to ruining
The times I had and the way I felt
Amidst your life and friends
Stop telling me that it's wrong
When my heart is on its mend

Everything has value
No matter how small
And the small stuff adds up
Sometimes greatest of all

You did not see through my eyes
Or feel through my heart
I am tied to the whole of it
Beyond your little part
The times I had and the way I felt
Amidst your life and friends
Stop telling me that it's wrong
When my heart is on its mend

You can't lessen the experiences I have
You can't destroy the feelings I feel
You can't cheapen the views I see
You can't make me any less real

SPOTLIGHT

Heated by lights that don't shine on me
Waiting for someone to see
But the lights are blinding in their face
They stand frozen in their place
I've shined my light on many friends
Happy to watch them grow
Watching their lives ebb and flow
All the while wishing secretly
That soon their light will shine on me.

THERAPY

Thought provoking conversation
Full of inspiration
Thought patterns changed in the blink of an eye
History revisited, reborn, then left out to die
New horrors revealed
After deep layers peeled
New light is shed
With these new thoughts in my head
Did something change? Will it last?
What's next? One can only ask.

LIVING UP

I saw a man who looked like you today
An ache overcame me
For fear I haven't lived up
To what you wanted me to be
I wonder still if you are watching
Over the group you began
And if you are pleased we still
Swim the waters you swam
Thoughts of you are constant
Bring my spirits up
For you touched me deeply
Dared me to drink from the cup
One that overfills still to this day
Because I knew you so long ago
And you propelled me
To stop fighting and never let go

SO LONG AGO

Just found out I lost you
So long ago
You told me you were moving, Ohio somewhere
Your new house, Heaven
I didn't know until now
So long ago
Did you spare me by speaking of joys?
My pain, now magnified
I lost you
So long ago
So long ago

BALD HEAD

A hat worn everyday
To prevent sunburn
Of face, shoulders, scalp
She always walked in
Confident
Smiling
Sometimes twirling
Sometimes dancing
Full of spirit

Not caring about
What she didn't have
For that mattered not

Each day greeted
With hope and drive

She was happy to be alive

MY STUFFED BEAR

There is this cutie pie
So lovable; doesn't lie
Gives hugs at every turn
Never expects any in return
Quiet, and ever so cuddly
Bestest friend one could ever be
Always there when I am sad
Takes away all the mad
Covered in pink fur from head to toe
Always my friend, never my foe
Puts a smile on my face
Even when I feel out of place
I love my bear and my bear loves me
When my bear is around, I am happy

CONVERSATION PIECE

When my friends arrive
They give me a look
Because on my table
Is a cupcake photo book
They can't figure out
Why it is there
Because a guy like me
Big as a bear
Shouldn't love something oh so sweet
These fancy cupcakes, oh so good
I took their photos
So that I always would
Remember the ones I liked the best
Before I ate them up
I keep the book on my table
Next to my favorite coffee cup
For my friends to see
As they arrive
So that our conversation
Will always thrive

CULTURAL

OBSERVATIONS

BEST FOOT FORWARD

Stepping out, dressed to the nines
Wondering if I'll conquer this time
After failing so many times before
Can I survive failure, even once more?
Resume in hand, smile on my face
Please tell me, am I in the right place?
Don't say I'm overqualified for this job
I work hard; am not a slob
I'll do whatever needs to be done
Please pick me as the ONE
I can't go back home, failed
Our future already derailed
The present is on shaky ground
Please help me turn it around

    I'm afraid to say sir/ma'am
    It is out of my hands
    I am so sorry I have to say
    The job was given away
    Thank you so much for your time
    Too bad you were so late in line
    There are so many with your pleas
    We can't hire everyone, don't you see?
    Your suit is nice; your resume grand
    I hope you can understand

Does it matter when I enter through the doors?
Is it my fault, or is it yours?
Stepping in, dressed for success
Wondering how I'm in this mess
Still failing, as before
Is it the suit I wore?

PROTESTING NOT!

There is this enemy with unknown might.
Courage failing to stand up and fight.
They are a shadowy, enemy. Hiding.
Various news reports always siding
with stories seemingly more profound
than threats this enemy throws around.
Polished anchors chatting about
certain celebrities' woes, giving clout -
lending more weight than these stories deserve
twisting words and views to serve,
a capitalist foundation, need,
a simple deadly sin: greed.
Who can believe reports given today,
changed tomorrow to keep at bay
fears that would eventually prevent
viewers to view the next event?

Ad sales will fall if truths are told:
So they don't report real news - ad time can't be
      sold...

DRUGS

I don't want babies,
      I take drugs.
I don't want pain,
      I take drugs.
I don't want insomnia,
      I take drugs.
I don't want illness,
      I take drugs.
I want life,
      I don't take drugs.

REFERENCE POINTS

Understanding comes from translation
Translation comes from a reference point
Without the beginning, or the end,
or even a middle
Information is lost, unusable
If you can't relate, or pull it in
It is because there was nowhere to begin
To translate that life to yours
Or that word into meaning
There must be a common thread to pull upon
Commonality which breeds understanding
Otherwise a speck of dust floating in a vacuum
Will hang forever in the void

WATCHING WATER BOIL

Watching pots to keep them cold
Never works when flames are bold
Burning hot through solid ice
Flames so high as to entice
Gather you in; burn your skin
Roiling boil never to cool
To tame the heat, such as fool
Watching pots to keep them cold
Never works when flames are bold

BUTTERFLY WINGS

They say a butterfly can start a tornado a half
     world away
But we never think of this as we go about our
     day
We never think of what affect we have in the
     world
The things we do are just there, hurled
Out into oblivion, no matter the effect on others
Until the weight of the world starts to smother
What difference in the world do I make
With every breath that I take?
What would have happened had I crashed my
     car?
Would the people hit still be who they are?
With their path changed, forever that day
Is the world changed in an irrevocable way?
What of the creativity that came of that choice
Did that become a heard voice
Or just some other dribble in a world full of
     noise
Or will it become a thing full of joys?
We all need to stop and think of what effect we
     exude
Into the world before it's screwed.

SPOILER ALERT

Let the story unfold.
Do not skip forward to reveal.
Knowing what is to come,
Makes the heart numb before it feels.
Let the story tell itself -
From beginning to end.
For there is meaning in the journey,
What the author intends.
Revel in the process
Of living in the moment
(Not in what comes next)
Sometimes now is now
And is purposed to perplex.
Don't give in
To what others know.
It may take the story for a ride
Where it wasn't supposed to go.

PROMPTED POETRY
TWEETSPEAK POETRY PROMPT - VERSION 1

1 - Surely someone, somewhere
2 - Understands what you're saying
3 - Under your layers of meaning

4 - Past the signs that say "beware"
5 - Along the path you are portraying
6 - With those words intervening

7 - Will start to stop and compare
8 - Their worlds with your conveying
9 - Those very thoughts that go careening

10 - And only then they will dare
11 - Something larger than displaying
12 - Defining a perfect gleaning

TWEETSPEAK POETRY PROMPT - VERSION 2

1 - Surely someone, somewhere
4 - Past the signs that say "beware"
7 - Will start to stop and compare
10 - And only then they will dare

2 - Understands what you're saying
5 - Along the path you are portraying
8 - Their worlds with your conveying
11 - Something larger than displaying

3 - Under your layers of meaning
6 - With those words intervening
9 - Those very thoughts that go careening
12 - Defining a perfect gleaning

TOO BUSY

Working, playing, eating, laughing
Too much to do in a day
Which part of your life do you give up
When "stuff" gets in the way?
Do you give up playing
In lieu of work?
Do you do it because
Your boss is a jerk?
Do you give up eating
To be sexy and thin?
Do you do it because
It is how you think you will win?
Do you give up laughter
In the face of pain?
Or do you put yourself first
And play in the rain?
Think about the choices you make
Don't be afraid of chances to take
Remember to put yourself first
Being too busy, is only a curse..

INSPIRATIONS

Where do they come from?
Where do they go?

Hitting like a freight train,
Stinging like a bee,
Floating like a butterfly,
The beauty of the tree.
Sunrise, sunset,
The moments in between.
Paintings, movies,
Sights not yet seen.
Silence, sirens,
The moments within a song.
Doing things right,
Still getting them wrong.
The feelings you have;
The feelings you won't.
The happiness you bring;
The quarrels you don't.
Soft rain proceeding
Thundering dark storms.
Rainbows and sunshine
When the weather turns warm.
Reality, insanity,
A very fine line defines.
Keeping to the rules,
Then coloring outside the lines.
Holding onto hope -
When all is lost.
Winning the game
With a hail Mary toss.

So fleeting, so haunting,

You never can know.....

So take your seeds and plant them all,
Some will grow weeds but others will grow tall.

While the tall ones grow strong with bright
      brilliant leaves,
Do not discount the power of weeds.
They teach you that you can't always win.
They toughen you up, to take one on the chin.
They teach you not to plant where they grow,
For they take advantage of all that you know.

IT BELONGS TO THE DAY

Where does the time go? Away.
Why can't we keep it? It belongs to the day.
Why can't we speed it up or slow it down?
It belongs to the day.
We are not its master.
Forever fleeting, always retreating.
Never ours to keep.
Years go by, days grow short,
Wrinkles get deep.
We watch it fly by when having fun,
Or fade away with the setting sun.
We ache as clocks tick the hours by,
When something dreadful is nearby.
Going to lunch,
Going to work,
Going to spend the day...
Even though it is never mine to pay.

GAMBLING PROBLEM

The only reason to gamble
Is a desire to win big
So when we retrace our steps
And try to relive
A gamble made to regain
What we once had in
Feelings, emotions, good times
Once we begin....
We see our gamble losing
Our forces compound
Our past rekindled
Cannot be found
A gamble made, lost
A lesson learned
Never bet at a losing place twice
You're bound to get burned

WATCHING, WAITING, WANTING, HOPING

Watching TV, some nonsensical show
About nothing of importance
Nothing I didn't know
Waiting for intelligence
To somehow appear
Within the context of stupidity
Like that commercial for beer
Hoping I don't find
What it is I seek
Because stupidity breeding brilliance
Means our intelligence has peaked
Wanting nothing more than sleep
After my mind has turned to mush
I didn't think about the caffeine
Still keeping me up
Watching, waiting, wanting, hoping
Trying, but not that hard
For something new to happen
To Someone new and smart

FEELING OLD

I stopped keeping up with the Jones'
Because they weren't interesting anymore
Then I stopped paying attention to the Smiths
Because they weren't hard core
Now I am looking around
Boy how the world has changed
Not liking what I am looking at
Everything seems so strange
There aren't any family values
No sense of dinner at 5
Everyone trying to out do another
To prove they are alive
It makes no sense to me
And now I feel my age
I want to put my blinders on
And wait for another way to gauge
The years I have lived
The knowledge I have gained
The morals I share
With the friends I have made

DO NOT REPEAT

Walking through a war scene
Crawling out of a ravine
To meet someone with images of gore
Reliving the Civil War
Through the passage of time, path up-kept
Tears, it seems, are still being wept
Places, times, and paths all marked
And with time, they are all remarked
So that people like me can walk through time
Relive the past, out of the ravine climb
To find ourselves alive and well
Out of the ravine known as hell
Luckier than the 700+ dead
Who took bullets to the head
Believing that their side was right
Wanting to help end the fight
Constantly marching towards their death
Tired, hungry, completely out of breath
I can't believe these men kept moving
When their situation was not improving
I would have stopped in my track
Turned, run, high tailed it back
But the men who died that faithful day
Kept on fighting, come what may
I mourn their deaths and their deeds
And pray that history does not repeat.

RINGING IN THE YEAR

Sitting here watching the evening pass
Waiting for the next year to start
Reading what others are saying
As the year begins to depart
Reliving things they have done
Or hoping for what next year will bring
All this seems so important
As the new year is about to ring
Why are we not like this on other days
In the middle of the year
When the calendar changes from June to July
What is it about January that brings this fear?

FOR PROTECTION

You keep your mouth shut
For Protection

You keep your eyes open
For Protection

You keep your ears listening
For Protection

You keep your body covered
For Protection

You keep your heart cold
For Protection

You keep your soul searching
For Protection

But are you overprotected?

CLOCKS

There aren't enough hours in the day
To get things to go my way
Now that I sit and think about time
And the lack that is always mine
I want to wind the clock too tight
So that it spins loose
Allowing every one who tells time
To feel they get to choose
What time it is or how much they get
To experience a life they won't forget

DEPTHS

I don't see things like you
You see surface; I see through
What wouldn't waste your time
Becomes cherished when mine
All those people, disregarded
I see them as brokenhearted
Please stop, stay awhile
See beyond their rank and file
Enjoy the world and the beauty within
Before your end begins

CONCEPT OF TIME

Watches, clocks, and sunshine
Decorations all
Because time doesn't matter
Not even to the clock on the wall
It speeds up, slows down
Sometimes even stands still
We can never control it
Try to overcome it, we will
But try as we might
We are doomed to fail
Because time continues to fly
No matter how loud we wail
So once we all realize
Changing time is for naught
It will matter no more
When our watch is forgot

ADS

Ads, ads everywhere
Trying to sell
Everything to everyone
Never can tell
What is real
What is deceit
Including the totals
Upon your receipt
The stories they portray
Nightly on the news
Seem to be developed
Just to help you choose
What to buy, where, why, when
And how much to pay
For the products you NEED to have
Each and every day
Appealing to our weakest link
Idolatry of self
So that we grab that item
Continuously off the shelf

CELL PHONE

Sitting in a room full of people
Completely alone

Because everyone has their attentions
Buried in their phone

Trying to garner attention
Enduring failure

Without desire
To fall victim to the lure

Giving up fitting in
Being alone

Watching everyone
Watching their phone

MONA LISA

Pictures snapping in front of the "NO PHOTOS"
    sign
People crowding instead of forming a line
Cramming closer, craning their necks to see
The most famous painting by Leonardo da Vinci

An alarm sounds, closer than they realize
Fear sets in when they hear painful cries
Eyes go wide, as blood drains from faces
Rational thought flees as they seek outdoor
    spaces
Trying to get out as the alarms still ring
Pulsing, thrusting, shoving, trampling

Bodies stuck within the frames
Packed in tight to escape the flames
Panicked cries fill the air
Scratching, clawing, pulling out hair
Bodies collapsing to the floor
Instead of walking calmly through the door

ROUSING APPLAUSE

The actors walked onstage
To perform in front of a doubting crowd
The words he spoke; the actions she took
Are only those that the director allowed

Making a point for the audience to take home
Within their minds, thoughts, and hearts
For when the actors take their bows
The play's many parts

Become whole

Before they left, the audience began to clap and
        scream
No longer full of doubt
They took to their feet in a great wave
Paying their respect before they went out

LIKE A GIRL #1

I never thought like a girl
Always surrounded by boys
I dressed like them, learned from them
Always played with their toys

The only differences that ever hit home
Were physical, unavoidable, undeniable
Yet I never saw myself as less than me
Always felt my friendships viable

I threw punches that blackened eyes
I hit fastballs our team's hitters missed
I ran faster than the boys I knew
Still held beauty that could be kissed

Sexual tensions taught me lust
Gave me confidence in a knowing trust

Having sisters throwing fits
Over hair, make-up, dresses and such
Made the boys laugh, ignore
Saying "girls are way too much"

As I heard what the boys said
I learned that all that "stuff"
Was just a wrapping around who I am
And as a person I am more than enough

As some girls left me in the wings
(Constantly surrounded by men)
They'd get jealous, throw mud
Somehow thinking they can win

These girls left me lonely in a way
"Such a tomboy at heart," the girls would say

Yet I never thought like a girl
Never have, never will
Because thinking like me
Has given my life such thrill

I repaired plumbing, painted walls, installed tiles
Learned to do my make up and use nail files
I fixed bikes, motorcycles and sometimes cars
Landing cherry drops off the monkey bars
I did everything that girls could do
And even the boys too
Don't fight like a girl
Hit like this
Don't slap, don't claw
Make a fist
Don't swing like a girl
Keep your eye on the ball
When you hit, get your butt on base
Run fast, but don't trip and fall
When I started winning better than them
They took pride because they taught me well
I wasn't held back, or pulled down
They lifted me up when I fell
Let's teach girls to think this way,
So brilliance will shine beyond today:
She can do everything the boys can do
Sometimes somewhat better too
All you have to do is give her a chance
And let her

FACE THE DAY

Doing my best to live in peace
Making myself beautiful
Inside and out
By filling my heart with love
Erasing all doubt
Everyday I wake up
To face the day
Smiling, happy, full of joy
I make my way
Through the twists and turns
Ups and downs
Past the hateful
Lifting spirits of all around

BAKING

A tablespoon of this, a teaspoon of that
A little bit of bliss, all tossed in a vat
Sugar and spice, everything nice
Snips and snails, and puppy dogs' tails
Mixing, blending a little at a time
"Use lemons, avoid the lime"
Recipes directing the work ahead
"Combine colors: blue, yellow, red"

Too much of this, too little of that
Not enough bliss, all tossed in a hat
The batter left in the oven too long
That is how the baker got it all wrong
The treat set out to be made, so divine
Appeared to rot somewhere along the line
"It doesn't look like the picture at all,"
Said the authorities who made the call

But didn't brownies and brittle occur
Because the recipe was a blur?
A little mistake here and there, became
        something more
Something people everywhere seem to adore
So even when the cake is flat as the pan
You might want to look deeper than
A picture of what the cake should be
Look deep enough to really see

Inspect each layer beyond the view
You might discover something new
A treat so divine, you cannot live without
Hidden behind a self-imposed cloud of doubt

NATURE POEMS

ALONE IN THE WOODS

The stars in the sky glow.
Bats fly to and fro.
You hear a trickling sound
As you lay on the ground.
The water flows over stones.
Somewhere near a bear groans.
The trees are tall and nearby.
Far off you hear a wolf cry.

Fear creeps over you in the dark.
You reach out and grab only bark.
Paranoia starts to settle in your head.
The fires die faster, now it's dead.
Someone's there; you can't act,
But you're seeing things, in fact.

An owl hoots, so you weep.
You wish yourself to sleep.

Soon comes the morning light,
And you're still awake with fright.

AUTUMN COLORS

In the Summer, these beautiful trees
Are green and glorious with all their leaves
But the Autumn lends such a better view
Oh such colors, changing hue
Blues from the sky, now clearly seen
And a little sprinkling of some evergreen
Reds, oranges and golds
And all the beauty they behold
Simmering sun with all of its light
Shining this day with all it's might
Browns from branches and quick little squirrels
Give motion to this quiet, little world
So inviting and quiet within
Please enjoy - dive right in!

FROZEN LAKE

Ice covers the nearby lake
Then disappears within a wake
It cracks, breaks then sinks below
The water's surface; now aglow
Reflecting sunlight throughout the day
Keeping less important thoughts at bay
For soon the sun will sink again
Bringing back the ice then
Crystals forming one by one
Playing their game, having fun
Before they crack, break, and sink
Leaving you again in the drink....

RIPPLE EFFECT

A pebble thrown
Into the lake
Creates a ripple
Amidst a wake
Each wave grows
Momentum abounds
Crashing ashore
Soaking the grounds

RAIN

The trees become
A player piano almost without sound
As their leaves are played by drops
Each note infinitely greater
The rain plays ferociously
Tempo gains momentum
The branches start dancing
Playing in the flashes
Like cameras on a red carpet
They are all played out by thunder
As the sun slips through the clouds

THE ENTERTAINER

"Boo" said the cat
When trying to scare the fish
Who didn't even flinch
The cat jumped down
Then jumped up again
To see if the fish would freak
It didn't
The cat watched the fish
Swim back and forth
Tail going one way
Head going the other

The whole time, entertaining
The fish

LIGHTNING STRIKE

Electricity runs wild
Ruining everything
It is too quiet without the noise
The underlying hum of the house
Gone
Burned up when the lightning
Tore through
Memories, entertainment, food
The wildness of the current
Was not contained
Rampant, wild, free
Gone

ICE STORM

The yard is littered
With bare trees bearing ice
Frozen, crystallized, majestic
As the sun rises above the ice-laden scene
The branches begin to shimmer
Rainbows captured within their glaze
Are cast upon the blanket of white
Laid over the dormant lawn
Even with life halted, stalled, cold
Throughout the littered bleakness
This beauty reminds

LIFE SPAN OF TWO CRAYONS

Two crayons, in a box of 16.
Along with Roy G. Biv (without the i)
And these other 8:
>Blue-green; blue-violet; brown; carnation
>pink; red-orange; red-violet; yellow-green;
>yellow-orange.
That was what they were to me in grade school.

Before I learned about lighting,
>Shading,
>>And blending.

In high school, they became the order and chaos
>of color.
Order viewed through a prism
>Or in the sky after storms pass.
Chaos, seeped through a coffee filter,
Brilliant in depth, turquoise and teals swirling
>across fibers
Overcoming every obstacle in its path.

By college they became bases:
>One deepened tones,
>One brightened.
>One slimmed,
>One reflected.
>One made my skin look sick, wan,
>>The other shrouded it in death.

My closet always had more of one than the
    other,
Especially after Labor Day.

Now, though, I am not so sure what these colors
    mean to me.
They are bleeding over the reds and blues
Dimming the stars that used to shine so bright.

I can no longer scratch beyond the surface,
Through the wax to see the colors hidden
    underneath,
The magic I recall of innocence, stolen.

No longer able to approach or understand one of
    these colors
Because God used the other.

Because even though these colors are
    Equal, Opposite
And when harmonious create the color best
    suited
    To display ALL colors of light

When they melted, they became
    Something different,
Took on a deadly shape
No longer able to color the world with their
    brilliance.

These two crayons are now
At the bottom of their graves.
Unmarked,
    Unworthy of everything,
        even their names.

Made in the USA
Columbia, SC
17 August 2022

65224558R00072